DISCLAIMER

By reading this disclaimer, you are accepting the terms of this disclaimer in full. If you disagree with this disclaimer, please do not order or read this book. The content in this book is provided for information and educational purposes only. Therefore this book is not intended to be used as a substitute for medical application whatsoever.

All products names, diet plans used in this book are for identification purposes only and are property of their respective owners. The use of these names does not imply endorsement. All other trademarks cited herein are the property of their respective owners.

None of the information in this book should be adopted as an independent medical or other professional advice. The information in this book has been compiled from different sources that are deemed reliable. Proper analysis and summary to the best of author's knowledge and belief has been done to achieve this book. However, the author cannot guarantee the accuracy and thus should not be held liable for any errors.

You acknowledge and agree that by continuing to read this book, you will (where applicable, appropriate, or necessary) consult a qualified medical professional on this information. The information in this book is not intended to be any sort of medical advice and should not be used in lieu of any medical advice by a licensed and qualified medical professional.

Lastly, do not interpret this book or its content for a medication. This is only a book guide. God bless you as you comply.

Copyright © 2023 by Maureen Doris (Ph.D)

All rights reserved. No part of this publication may be reproduced, distributed, or transmitted in any form or by any means, including photocopying, recording, or other electronic or mechanical methods, without the prior written permission of the publisher, except in the case of brief quotations embodied in critical reviews and certain other noncommercial uses permitted by copyright law.

The purpose of this book is to assist readers become well informed healthcare consumers. It is provided as overall health care advice.

It is always suggested that you seek medical advice from your personal physician before starting any fresh workout program.

This book is not designed to be a replacement for a certified physician's medical recommendation. In all issues pertaining to his / her health, the reader should check with their doctor. **Note:** This is a book and not a product. Be guided!

Table of Contents

DISCLAIMER 1
INTRODUCTION 8
    What Are FODMAPs? 8
    Benefits of a Low-FODMAP Diet 10
    Who Should Follow a Low-FODMAP DIET? 12
    Things to Do Before Starting Low-FODMAP Diet 13
    How to Follow a Low-FODMAP Diet 16
    Foods High in FODMAPs (and what to eat instead) 24
        Wheat 24
        Garlic 25
        Onion 27
        Fruit 28
        Vegetables 29
        Legumes and Pulses 30
        Sweeteners 32
        Other Grains 33
        Dairy 34
        Beverages 35
    What If Your Symptoms Don't Improve? 36
    A Low-FODMAP Diet Can Be Flavorful 38
    A Low-FODMAP Shopping List 41
    Guide to low FODMAP label reading 44

Can Vegetarians Follow a Low-FODMAP Diet?......................47
Delicious Low FODMAP Vegetarian Snacks and Recipes........53
    Vegetarian Curry Puffs..53
    Savory Crackers...57
    No Bake Protein Balls...59
    Ingredients..59
    Zucchini and Carrot Slice..60
Other Recipes...62
    Chocolate Cardamom Easter Buns..62
    Chocolate Pound Cake...65
    Citrus Pound Cake..68
    Condensed Milk Pound Cake..70
    Cinnamon Tea Cupcakes with Meringue Icing......................73
    Mixed Berry Sponge..76
    Carrot Cake Cupcakes..78
    St Clements Bundt Cake..81
    Lemon, Yogurt and Lemon Thyme Bundt Cake....................84
    Chocolate Bundt with Ganache..87
    Vegan Blueberry Pancakes...90
    Vegan Chocolate Peanut Butter Cookies................................92
    Vegan Beetroot Brownies...94
    Chocolate Chip Monster Cookies..96
    Spooky Halloween Brownies...98

Choc Hot Cross Buns 101

Chicken Tortilla's 105

Chunky Beef Pie 109

Pita Pockets with Pumpkin and Walnut Dip 113

Gnocchi 117

Pretzels 122

Chicken and Tomato Pasta Sauce 125

Sausage Rolls 127

A comprehensive table for some foods and their FODMAPs
.... 130

INTRODUCTION

Food is a common trigger of digestive symptoms. Interestingly, restricting certain foods can dramatically improve these symptoms in sensitive people.

In particular, a diet low in fermentable carbs known as FODMAPS is clinically recommended for the management of irritable bowel syndrome (IBS). This book explains what a low-FODMAP diet is, how it works and who should try it.

What Are FODMAPs?

FODMAP stands for fermentable oligo-, di-, mono-saccharides and polyols. These are the scientific terms used to classify groups of carbs that are notorious for triggering digestive symptoms like bloating, gas and stomach pain. In other words, FODMAPs are a group of fermentable carbs that aggravate gut symptoms in sensitive people. They're found in a wide range of foods.

FODMAPs are found in a wide range of foods in varying amounts. Some foods contain just one type, while others contain several.

The main dietary sources of the four groups of FODMAPs include:

1. Oligosaccharides: Wheat, rye, legumes and various fruits and vegetables, such as garlic and onions.
2. Disaccharides: Milk, yogurt and soft cheese. Lactose is the main carb.
3. Monosaccharides: Various fruit including figs and mangoes, and sweeteners such as honey and agave nectar. Fructose is the main carb.
4. Polyols: Certain fruits and vegetables including blackberries and lychee, as well as some low-calorie sweeteners like those in sugar-free gum.

Benefits of a Low-FODMAP Diet

A low-FODMAP diet restricts high-FODMAP foods. The benefits of a low-FODMAP diet have been tested in thousands of people with IBS across more than 30 studies. There is convincing evidence for the benefits of a low-FODMAP diet. The diet appears to improve digestive symptoms in approximately 70% of adults with IBS.

1. Reduced Digestive Symptoms

IBS digestive symptoms can vary widely, including stomach pain, bloating, reflux, flatulence and bowel urgency.

Stomach pain is a hallmark of the condition, and bloating has been found to affect more than 80% of people with IBS. Needless to say, these symptoms can be debilitating. One large study even reported that people with IBS said they would give up an average of 25% of their remaining lives to be symptom-free Fortunately, both stomach pain and bloating have been shown to significantly decrease with a low-FODMAP diet.

Evidence from four high-quality studies concluded that if you follow a low-FODMAP diet, your odds of improving stomach pain and bloating are 81% and 75% greater, respectively

Several other studies have suggested the diet can help manage flatulence, diarrhea and constipation.

2. Increased Quality of Life

People with IBS often report a reduced quality of life, and severe digestive symptoms have been associated with this. Luckily, the low-FODMAP diet improves overall quality of life. A low-FODMAP diet may increase energy levels in people with IBS, but placebo-controlled studies are needed to support this finding.

Who Should Follow a Low-FODMAP DIET?

A low-FODMAP diet is not for everyone. Unless you have been diagnosed with IBS, research suggests the diet could do more harm than good.

A low-FODMAP diet is recommended for adults with IBS. The evidence for its use in other conditions is limited and may do more harm than good. This is because most FODMAPs are prebiotics, meaning they support the growth of good gut bacteria.

Also, most of the research has been in adults. Therefore, there is limited support for the diet in children with IBS.

If you have IBS, consider this diet if you:

1. Have ongoing gut symptoms.
2. Haven't responded to stress management strategies.

3. Haven't responded to first-line dietary advice, including restricting alcohol, caffeine, spicy food and other common trigger foods

That said, there is some speculation that the diet may benefit other conditions, including diverticulitis and exercise-induced digestive issues.

It is important to be aware that the diet is an involved process. For this reason, it's not recommended to try it for the first time while traveling or during a busy or stressful period.

Things to Do Before Starting Low-FODMAP Diet

Before you embark on the low-FODMAP diet, there are several things you need to do. These simple steps will help increase your chances of successfully managing your digestive symptoms.

Make Sure You Actually Have IBS

Digestive symptoms can occur in many conditions, some harmless and others more serious.

Unfortunately, there is no positive diagnostic test to confirm you have IBS. For this reason, it is recommended you see a doctor to rule out more serious conditions first, such as celiac disease, inflammatory bowel disease and colon cancer

Once these are ruled out, your doctor can confirm you have IBS using the official IBS diagnostic criteria you must fulfill all three to be diagnosed with IBS

1. Recurrent stomach pain: On average, at least one day per week in the last three months.
2. Stool symptoms: These should match two or more of the following: related to defecation, associated with a change in frequency of

stool or associated with a change in the appearance of stool.
3. Persistent symptoms: Criteria fulfilled for the last three months with symptom onset at least six months before diagnosis.

Try First-Line Diet Strategies

The low-FODMAP diet is a time and resource-intensive process. This is why in clinical practice it is considered second-line dietary advice and is only used in a subset of people with IBS who don't respond to first-line strategies.

Plan Ahead

The diet can be difficult to follow if you are not prepared. Here are some tips:

- **Find out what to buy:** Ensure you have access to credible low-FODMAP food lists.
- **Get rid of high-FODMAP foods:** Clear your fridge and pantry of these foods.

- **Make a shopping list:** Create a low-FODMAP shopping list before heading to the grocery store, so you know which foods to purchase or avoid.
- **Read menus in advance:** Familiarize yourself with low-FODMAP menu options so you'll be prepared when dining out.

How to Follow a Low-FODMAP Diet

There are processes to follow in the when starting the FODMAP. Each stage is equally important in achieving long-term symptom relief and overall health and well-being.

Find a trained professional

All of the research to date on the diet indicates that the best results are achieved when you get support from a qualified dietary professional who is well-versed in the diet. A dietitian or health coach is important because:

1. You need to make sure that you are eating a wide variety of foods to ensure that you are taking in your daily nutritional requirements.
2. It will be helpful to have support as you learn to integrate the diet into your life.
3. They can help you best determine which of the FODMAP types are problematic for you.

Start a Food Diary

As you work through the various phases of the diet, you will want to keep a food diary. This will help you get a better sense of the relationship between the foods that you eat and the symptoms that you experience. This step will be especially helpful as you work through the various phases of the diet.

A food diary doesn't have to be anything fancy. You just want to keep track of everything you have eaten, what symptoms you are experiencing, and any other factors that might be affecting how you feel, such as stress, your menstrual cycle, etc.

Gather Your Resources

It can be very challenging to remember which foods are low in FODMAPs and which foods are high in FODMAPs and just as challenging to find the right foods to eat. Luckily, the success of the diet has spurred the development of available resources. The more food options you have, the more likely you will be to comply with the diet's guidelines.

Start the Restriction Process

This stage involves strict avoidance of all high-FODMAP foods. People who follow this diet often think they should avoid all FODMAPs long-term, but this stage should only last about 3-8 weeks. This is because it's important to include FODMAPs in the diet for gut health. This includes foods from the following FODMAP sub groups

- Fructans (found in some fruits, grains, nuts, and vegetables)

- Fructose (found in some fruits)
- GOS (found in beans, chickpeas, and lentils)
- Lactose (found in some dairy products)
- Polyols (found in some fruits, vegetables, and artificial sweeteners)

Some people notice an improvement in symptoms in the first week, while others take the full eight weeks. Once you have adequate relief of your digestive symptoms, you can progress to the next stage.

Slowly introduce FODMAPS back into your diet

This stage involves systematically reintroducing high-FODMAP foods. After you have hopefully enjoyed a significant decrease in symptoms, it is time to slowly re-introduce some foods back into your diet. For this reintroduction phase, it is recommended that you pick one FODMAP sub-group at a time to assess the effect of each group on your body. Your dietary professional can help you to figure out what foods you can test your sensitivity on. Plan to test each group for a week before moving onto the next group. Start with small amounts of foods so as to not cause severe symptoms.

If you experience no symptoms in response to your challenge foods, you can slowly start to increase the quantity you are eating. If you continue to tolerate the food, then you can conclude that you are not reactive to that particular sub-group and you can continue onto the next group.

If you experience symptoms, you can try to test a different food from within the same sub-group. If you continue to have a reaction, you should go back to the elimination diet for one week before moving on to the next sub-group.

After you have tested all sub-groups and have been relatively symptom-free for some time, you will want to re-test small amounts of the sub-group that you were initially reactive to. Once you have a good sense of which FODMAPs you are most reactive to, you can organize your diet so as to eat predominantly low-FODMAP, with minimal consumption of high-FODMAP foods. The goal is to keep your exposure to FODMAPs in a range that does not cause you to experience symptoms.

The purpose of this is twofold:

1. To identify which types of FODMAPs you tolerate. Few people are sensitive to all of them.
2. To establish the amount of FODMAPs you can tolerate. This is known as your "threshold level."

It is recommended that you undertake this step with a trained dietitian who can guide you through the appropriate foods. It is also important to remember that, unlike people with most food allergies, people with IBS can tolerate small amounts of FODMAPs.

Lastly, although digestive symptoms can be debilitating, they will not cause long-term damage to your body.

Personalization

This stage is also known as the "modified low-FODMAP diet." In other words, you still restrict some FODMAPs. However, the amount and type are tailored to your personal tolerance.

It is important to progress to this final stage in order to increase diet variety and flexibility. These qualities are linked with improved long-term compliance, quality of life and gut health.

Keep testing your range of foods

The low-FODMAP diet is not designed to be a "forever" diet. Many foods that are high in FODMAPs are also foods that can be very good for your health.

There are some concerns that FODMAP restriction can have a negative impact on your gut flora. The best thing for both your overall and your digestive health is to eat as wide a variety of healthy foods that you can.

There is some evidence that once you have followed the low-FODMAP diet you will improve your ability to tolerate previously troublesome foods. Therefore, you will want to be sure to keep re-introducing new foods into your diet at regular intervals to see if your sensitivities have changed. One helpful way is to set a reminder in your day planner or on your smartphone to go through the reintroduction phase again every three months

Foods High in FODMAPs (and what to eat instead)

Food is a common trigger of digestive issues. In particular, foods that are high in fermentable carbs can cause symptoms like gas, bloating and stomach pain.

A group of these carbs is known as FODMAPs, and foods can be classified as either high or low in these carbs.

Restricting high-FODMAP foods can provide remarkable relief of gut symptoms, particularly in people with irritable bowel syndrome (IBS).

Wheat

Wheat is one of the single biggest contributors of FODMAPs in the Western diet; however, it can be replaced with other, low-FODMAP whole grains. This is because wheat is consumed in large quantities not because it is a concentrated source of

FODMAPs. Wheat is the main source of FODMAPs in the Western diet.

In fact, wheat contains one of the lowest amounts of FODMAPs by weight. For this reason, foods that contain wheat as a minor ingredient, such as thickeners and flavorings, are considered low-FODMAP. The most common sources of wheat include bread, pasta, breakfast cereals, biscuits, and pastries.

Suggested low-FODMAP swaps for wheat are: Brown rice, buckwheat, maize, millet, oats, polenta, quinoa and tapioca.

Garlic

Garlic is one of the most concentrated sources of FODMAPs. However, garlic has many health benefits and should only be restricted in FODMAP-sensitive people.

Unfortunately, restricting garlic in your diet is notoriously difficult because it's added to many sauces, gravies and flavorings. In processed food, garlic may be listed among the ingredients as flavoring or natural flavor. Therefore, you need to avoid these ingredients if you are following a strict low-FODMAP diet. Fructans are the main type of FODMAP in garlic.

However, the quantity of fructans depends on whether the garlic is fresh or dried, as dried garlic contains about three times as many fructans as fresh garlic. Despite being high in FODMAPs, garlic is associated with many health benefits. This is why it should only be avoided in FODMAP-sensitive people.

Suggested low-FODMAP swaps for garlic are: Chives, chili, fenugreek, ginger, lemongrass, mustard seeds, saffron and turmeric.

Onion

Onions are another concentrated source of fructans. Different onion varieties contain different amounts of FODMAPs, but all onions are considered to contain high amounts.

Similar to garlic, onion is commonly used to flavor a wide range of dishes, making it difficult to restrict. Shallots are one of the highest sources of fructans, while a Spanish onion is one of the lowest sources. While different varieties of onions contain different amounts of FODMAPs, all onions are considered high-FODMAP.

Suggested low-FODMAP swaps for onions are: Asafoetida is a pungent spice commonly used in Indian cooking. It should be cooked in hot oil first and added in small amounts.

Fruit

All fruits contain the FODMAP fructose. However, some fruits have less fructose and can be enjoyed in single portions throughout the day. But interestingly, not all fruits are considered high in FODMAPs. This is because some fruits contain less fructose than others.

Also, some fruits contain high amounts of glucose, which is a non-FODMAP sugar. This is important because glucose helps your body absorb fructose.

This is why fruits that are high in both fructose and glucose do not typically cause gut symptoms. It's also why only fruits with more fructose than glucose are considered high-FODMAP. Nevertheless, even low-FODMAP fruits can cause gut symptoms if they're consumed in large quantities. This has to do with the total fructose load in your gut.

Therefore, sensitive people are encouraged to only eat one portion of fruit per sitting, or approximately 3 ounces (80 grams).

High-FODMAP fruits include: Apples, apricots, cherries, figs, mangoes, nectarines, peaches, pears, plums and watermelon

Low-FODMAP fruits include: Unripe bananas, blueberries, kiwi, limes, mandarins, oranges, papaya, pineapple, rhubarb and strawberries

Vegetables

Some vegetables are high in FODMAPs. Vegetables contain a diverse range of FODMAPs. However, many vegetables are naturally low in FODMAPs. In fact, vegetables contain the most diverse range of FODMAPs. This includes fructans, galacto-oligosaccharides (GOS), fructose, mannitol and sorbitol.

Furthermore, several vegetables contain more than one type of FODMAP. For example, asparagus contains fructans, fructose and mannitol. It's important to remember that vegetables are part of a healthy diet, and there is no need to stop eating them. Instead, simply switch out high-FODMAP vegetables for low-FODMAP ones.

High-FODMAP vegetables include: Asparagus, Brussels sprouts, cauliflower, chicory leaves, globe and Jerusalem artichokes, karela, leeks, mushrooms and snow peas

Low-FODMAP vegetables include: Bean sprouts, capsicum, carrot, choy sum, eggplant, kale, tomato, spinach and zucchini

Legumes and Pulses

Legumes and pulses are notorious for causing excess gas and bloating, which is partly attributed to their high FODMAP content which can be altered by how they are prepared. The key FODMAP in legumes and pulses is called galacato-oligosaccharides (GOS).

The GOS content of legumes and pulses is affected by how they are prepared. For instance, canned lentils contain half the GOS than boiled lentils do. This is because GOS is water-soluble, meaning some of it leaches out of the lentils and into the liquid.

Nonetheless, even canned legumes are a significant source of FODMAPs, though small portions (typically 1/4 cup per serving) can be included in a low-FODMAP diet.

Legumes and pulses are good sources of protein for vegetarians, but they are not the only choice. There are many other low-FODMAP, protein-rich options.

High-FODMAP legumes and pulses include: Baked beans, black-eyed peas, broad beans, butter beans, chickpeas, kidney beans, lentils, soybeans and split peas

Low-FODMAP, vegetarian sources of protein include: Tofu, eggs and most nuts and seeds.

Sweeteners

Sweeteners can be a hidden source of FODMAPs, as adding sweeteners to a low-FODMAP food can increase its overall FODMAP content.

High-FODMAP sweeteners can increase a food's FODMAP content. To avoid these hidden sources, check the ingredients list on packaged foods. To avoid these hidden sources, check the ingredients list on packaged foods.

Alternatively, if you're in the UK, the King's College low-FODMAP app allows you to scan the barcodes on packaged foods to detect high-FODMAP foods.

High-FODMAP sweeteners include: Agave nectar, high-fructose corn syrup, honey and added polyols in sugar-free mints and chewing gums (check the labels for sorbitol, mannitol, xylitol or isomalt)

Low-FODMAP sweeteners include: Glucose, maple syrup, sucrose, sugar and most artificial sweeteners like aspartame, saccharin and Stevia.

Other Grains

Wheat is not the only grain high in FODMAPs. In fact, other grains like rye contain nearly twice the number of FODMAPs as wheat does. However, the FODMAP content of grains can be reduced through different processing methods.

That being said, some types of rye bread, such as sourdough rye bread, can be low in FODMAPs.

This is because the process of making sourdough involves a fermentation step, during which some of its FODMAPs are broken down into digestible sugars. This step has been shown to reduce its fructan content by more than 70%. This reinforces the notion that specific processing methods can alter the FODMAP content of food.

High-FODMAP grains include: Amaranth, barley and rye.

Low-FODMAP grains include: Brown rice, buckwheat, maize, millet, oats, polenta, quinoa and tapioca.

Dairy

Dairy products are the main source of the FODMAP lactose but a surprising number of dairy foods are naturally low in lactose.

However, not all dairy foods contain lactose. This includes many hard and matured kinds of cheese, as much of their lactose is lost during the cheese making process.

But it's important to remember that some cheeses contain added flavorings, such as garlic and onion that make them high FODMAP.

High-FODMAP dairy foods include: Cottage cheese, cream cheese, milk, quark, ricotta and yogurt.

Low-FODMAP dairy foods include: Cheddar cheese, cream, feta cheese, lactose-free milk and Parmesan cheese.

Beverages

Beverages are another key source of FODMAPs. Many beverages are high in FODMAPs, and this is not limited to beverages made from high-FODMAP ingredients. In fact, beverages made from low-FODMAP ingredients can also be high in FODMAPs.

Orange juice is one example. While oranges are low-FODMAP, many oranges are used to make one glass of orange juice, and their FODMAP content is additive. Furthermore, some types of tea and alcohol are also high in FODMAPs.

High-FODMAP beverages include: Chai tea, chamomile tea, coconut water, dessert wine and rum.

Low-FODMAP beverages include: Black tea, coffee, gin, green tea, peppermint tea, vodka, water and white tea

What If Your Symptoms Don't Improve?

The low-FODMAP diet does not work for everyone with IBS. Around 30% of people don't respond to the diet. However, there are common mistakes worth checking before you try other therapies.

Fortunately, there are other non-diet-based therapies that may help. Talk to your doctor about alternative options. That said, before you give up on the low-FODMAP diet, you should:

Check and Recheck Ingredient Lists

Prepackaged foods often contain hidden sources of FODMAPs.

Common culprits include onion, garlic, sorbitol and xylitol which can trigger symptoms even in small amounts.

Consider the Accuracy of Your FODMAP Information

There are many low-FODMAP food lists available

Think about Other Life Stressors

Diet is not the only thing that can aggravate IBS symptoms. Stress is another major contributor. In fact, no matter how effective your diet, if you are under severe stress, your symptoms are likely to persist.

NOTE: The low-FODMAP diet can dramatically improve digestive symptoms, including those in people with IBS.

However, not everyone with IBS responds to the diet. What's more, the diet involves a three-stage process that can take up to six months.

And unless you need it, the diet may do more harm than good, since FODMAPs are prebiotics that support the growth of beneficial bacteria in your gut. Nonetheless, this diet could be truly life-changing for those struggling with IBS.

A Low-FODMAP Diet Can Be Flavorful

Several popular flavors are high in FODMAPs, but there are many low-FODMAP herbs and spices that can be used to make flavorsome meals.

Garlic and onion are both very high in FODMAPs. This has led to the common misconception that a low-FODMAP diet lacks flavor. While many recipes do use onion and garlic for flavor, there are many low-FODMAP herbs, spices and savory flavorings that can be substituted instead. It is also worth highlighting that you can still get the flavor from garlic using strained garlic-infused oil, which is low in FODMAPs. This is because the FODMAPs in garlic are not fat-soluble, meaning the garlic flavor is transferred to the oil, but the FODMAPs aren't.

Try adding the following ingredients to enhance the flavor of your meals, without aggravating IBS symptoms.

- Asafetida powder pinch only for onion flavor
- Chives
- Fresh herbs such as parsley, coriander, thyme, basil and rosemary
- Garlic infused oil

How to achieve

1. Peel and cut garlic into large pieces.

2. Saute in oil for 1-2 minutes to develop flavor in the oil.

3. Discard pieces of garlic.

- Ginger
- Lemon juice
- Lime juice
- Maple syrup
- Salt and pepper
- Spices (such as cumin, coriander, turmeric (avoid seasoning mixes/blends)
- Spring onions (green part only)
- Stock (made without onions/garlic)
- Fenugreek
- Mustard seed
- Saffron
- Turmeric

- Pepper
- Lemon grass
- Chilli

Note - chili also contains capsaisin, a natural ingredient which may trigger symptoms in some people with IBS. Limit your intake if chili aggravates your IBS symptoms

A Low-FODMAP Shopping List

Many foods are naturally low in FODMAPs. Many foods are naturally low in FODMAPs. That said, many processed foods have added FODMAPs and should be limited.

Many doctors are now routinely recommending the low-FODMAP diet to their IBS patients. This is because the diet is the first food-based treatment that has research support for effectively reducing IBS symptoms of gas, bloating, diarrhea and constipation. With good compliance and support, approximately 70 percent of IBS patients will experience significant symptom relief.

The diet is a bit tricky and will require a commitment on your part to ensure that you are choosing foods consistent with the diet. Therefore you will not want to take on the diet during a time when you will be extra busy or have limited time in your schedule for food prep and packing.

Here is a simple shopping list to get you started.

- Protein: Beef, chicken, eggs, fish, lamb, pork, prawns and tofu
- Whole grains: Brown rice, buckwheat, maize, millet, oats and quinoa
- Fruit: Bananas, blueberries, kiwi, limes, mandarins, oranges, papaya, pineapple, rhubarb and strawberries
- Vegetables: Bean sprouts, bell peppers, carrots, choy sum, eggplant, kale, tomatoes, spinach and zucchini

- Nuts: Almonds (no more than 10 per sitting), macadamia nuts, peanuts, pecans, pine nuts and walnuts
- Seeds: Linseeds, pumpkin, sesame and sunflower
- Dairy: Cheddar cheese, lactose-free milk and Parmesan cheese
- Oils: Coconut oil and olive oil
- Beverages: Black tea, coffee, green tea, peppermint tea, water and white tea
- Condiments: Basil, chili, ginger, mustard, pepper, salt, white rice vinegar and wasabi powder

Additionally, it's important to check the ingredients list on packaged foods for added FODMAPs.

Food companies may add FODMAPs to their foods for many reasons, including as prebiotics, as a fat substitute or as a lower-calorie substitute for sugar.

Guide to low FODMAP label reading

Reading food labels can be a tricky business, but decoding them whilst following the Low FODMAP Diet can be even more distressing.

Whether you're eating out, searching for a sauce, or are in a rush on your lunch break and need to grab something quick, FODMAPs are present in so many different prepared foods and it can be hard to know where to begin. Ingredient lists are often a full paragraph long and regularly contain different and rather complicated chemical names, leaving you confused, frustrated and more likely to give up and grab something you shouldn't.

So what can you do to help make it easier?

The list of high FODMAP ingredients commonly found in prepared foods is a long one, so instead of overwhelming yourself trying to remember every possibility, start by being aware of these most common high FODMAP culprits:

- Sweeteners such as honey, high fructose corn syrup and agave
- Wheat, barley or rye
- Sugar alcohols ending in '-ol' such as sorbitol, mannitol and xylitol
- Onion and garlic, as well as onion/garlic salt or powder. Packets might also have 'spices', 'natural flavors', or 'flavors'' written vaguely
- Fibers including inulin and chicory root
- Fruit juice concentrates, or purees made from high FODMAP foods such as apples or pears

Items such as cereal bars, pre-prepared sandwiches or ready meals, chewing gums, medicines, sauces, stocks, yogurts, 'free-from' products, marinated meats, breakfast cereals and jams are often common sources of sneaky high FODMAP ingredients. Take extra care when looking at the labels of these.

Remember that ingredients on food labels are listed in order of weight. So the first ingredient listed is in the highest quantity and the last ingredient listed is in the lowest quantity. When your gut is feeling better and you're starting to re-introduce higher FODMAP foods, you may choose to eat products which have high FODMAP ingredients such as onion powder listed right near the end. As always, it's recommended to go slowly and try foods that are new to you in small amounts to see how you tolerate them. It might be delicious but you can eat more later

Whilst label reading is a really important way to spot FODMAPs, be aware that high FODMAP ingredients aren't always easy to identify. Even if you find a product that looks like it would be safe, go easy and use trial and error to confirm that you are able to tolerate it.

Look out for products that are certified Low FODMAP

Don't expect to be a perfect shopper from the start! If you're new to the Low FODMAP Diet, be patient with yourself and allow extra time for label reading when you're out grocery shopping or picking up some lunch on the go. Over time reading labels will become easier and you'll build up a bank of go-to products you know work for you and your gut.

Can Vegetarians Follow a Low-FODMAP Diet?

There are many protein-rich vegetarian options suitable for a low-FODMAP diet. Therefore, there is no reason why a vegetarian with IBS cannot follow a well-balanced low-FODMAP diet.

A well-balanced vegetarian diet can be low in FODMAPs. Nonetheless, following a low-FODMAP diet if you are a vegetarian can be more challenging. This is because high-FODMAP legumes are staple protein foods in vegetarian diets. That said, you can include small portions of canned and rinsed legumes in a low-FODMAP diet. Serving sizes are typically about 1/4 cup (64 grams).

There are also many low-FODMAP, protein-rich options for vegetarians, including tempeh, tofu, eggs, Quorn (a meat substitute) and most nuts and seeds. If you are a vegetarian and looking to try a low FODMAP diet for IBS, With a few considerations, it is possible to follow a nutritionally-balanced low FODMAP vegetarian diet.

These tips will help you

1. Seek out expert help.

Working with a FODMAP-trained registered dietitian can be beneficial for anyone following a low FODMAP diet, but it can be especially helpful if you are also following a vegetarian or vegan lifestyle. One of the biggest problems people can face on the low FODMAP diet is the lack of diversity in their diet and lack of balanced meals. A trained dietitian can help you easily navigate the low FODMAP diet, avoid unnecessary food restrictions, and prevent potential nutrient deficiencies.

2. Focus on low FODMAP foods with key nutrients.

With proper planning, it is possible to eat a nutritionally-balanced low FODMAP vegetarian diet. A few of the nutrients requiring extra attention when following a low FODMAP vegetarian diet include protein, iron, and calcium.

Protein

Legumes like beans, lentils, and soybeans are common sources of protein for many vegetarians. Many of these legumes are high in FODMAPs and limited on the low FODMAP diet. Fortunately, there are other low FODMAP vegetarian protein options to choose from which includes

- Firm tofu and tempeh
- Lactose-free milk and yogurt
- Low lactose cheeses like cheddar, feta, and Swiss
- Peanut butter
- Nuts like walnuts, pecans, and macadamias
- Seeds like chia, flax, hemp, pumpkin, and sunflower
- Whole grains like quinoa, brown rice, and polenta

- Eggs

Some forms of processing can help reduce the FODMAP content of some FODMAP-containing foods. For example, canned chickpeas and lentils have lower FODMAP levels than chickpeas and lentils that were cooked from scratch.

Iron

The plant-based form of iron (non-heme iron) is not absorbed as efficiently as iron from animal sources (heme iron). You can increase the absorption of plant-based iron by pairing it with a low FODMAP source of vitamin C like oranges, kiwifruit, strawberries, bell peppers, or tomatoes. Some low FODMAP vegetarian sources of iron include:

- Firm tofu and tempeh
- Spinach
- Pumpkin seeds

- Quinoa
- Canned lentils and chickpeas
- Eggs

Calcium

Lactose-free milk products are low in FODMAPs and can help you meet your calcium needs. If dairy is not a part of your diet, include plant-based alternatives that are low in FODMAPs like fortified almond milk, firm tofu, and dark leafy greens like kale, spinach, and collard greens.

Delicious Low FODMAP Vegetarian Snacks and Recipes.

Vegetarian Curry Puffs

Preparation: 1 hour

Cooking: 20 mins

Makes: 24

Low FODMAP serving: 2

Ingredients

For the pastry

- 300g All Purpose/ Plain Flour
- 125g butter, cubed
- 125g water
- 1 teaspoon salt
- 1 teaspoon baking powder
- 500ml vegetable oil

For the filling

- 1teaspoon garlic infused olive oil

- 400g potato
- 300g pumpkin
- 300g spinach
- 2teaspoon curry powder (with no garlic or onion)
- 1 leek (green part only)
- 200g broccoli florets

Process

1. Combine the flour, baking powder and salt in a large bowl then rub the butter into the flour using your hands or an electric mixer with a paddle attachment until it forms a fine crumb.
2. Add in the water 1 tbsp. at a time while mixing on medium speed for 5 minutes to form dough.
3. Tip out onto a floured surface and then knead dough for 5 min until it springs back at

touch. Cover and rest for at least 30 minutes in the fridge.

4. While the dough is resting heat the garlic infused olive oil in large pan, then add in the potatoes and pumpkin and cook for 10 minutes or until they are just soft. Add in the leek and cook on high for 2 minutes then add in the broccoli, spinach and curry powder. Set aside.
5. Cut the dough into 24 even sized bits. On a floured surface roll one piece of dough out into a 2 mm thick circle (about 7 inch in diameter).
6. Place a tbsp. of filling into the center of the dough. Bring the edges together and fold them over each other pinching the dough with your hands to form a seal. Repeat with remaining dough.
7. Heat the vegetable oil in a heavy based pan. It is hot enough when small bubbles start to

form around the base of a wooden spoon. Lower a curry puff into the oil using a slotted spoon – be careful not to splash the oil as it is very hot.

8. Cook for 1-2 minutes on each side or until golden brown. Use the slotted spoon to drain excess oil and then place cooked curry puff on a piece of paper towel to further drain oil and cool slightly. You can also bake the curry puffs at 180 C for 35 minutes with an egg wash on top if preferred.
9. Serve with FODMAP friendly sweet chili sauce or tzatziki.

Savory Crackers

Preparation: 5 minutes

Baking: 15 minutes

Makes: 40 crackers depending on the shape and size of the crackers

Low FODMAP serving: 4 crackers

Ingredients

- 1 ¼ cup (150g) all Purpose/Plain Flour
- 2 teaspoon (7g) poppy seeds
- 1 teaspoon (3g) Nigella seeds
- 1 teaspoon (4.5g) wholegrain mustard
- 1 teaspoon (1.5g) dried mixed herbs
- 1 teaspoon (7g) salt
- 4 tablespoons (60g) Unsalted Butter, softened and cubed
- ¼ cup (65g) water
- 1 tablespoon (25g) maple syrup

- 1 (55g) XL Egg, lightly beaten

Process

1. Preheat fan-forced oven to 205°C (400°F), and line a baking tray with baking paper.
2. Combine the dry ingredients in a large bowl and rub butter into the mix.
3. Add the water and maple syrup, mixing until dough is formed.
4. Lightly flour work surface and transfer dough onto the surface.
5. Roll out the dough until very thin (approx. 1/8th inch). You may want to do this on your baking tray.
6. Cut dough, or roll out in a rectangle shape for baking. Brush each cracker lightly with the beaten egg for a golden finish when baked.
7. Bake for 12-15 minutes or until golden brown.
8. Allow to cool for 10 minutes.

No Bake Protein Balls

Preparation: 10 minutes

Makes: 10-12 balls

Low FODMAP serving: 2 balls

Ingredients

- ½ cup (150g) Peanut Butter, smooth
- ¼ cup (150g) whey protein isolate
- ¼ cup (32g) all Purpose/Plain Flour
- 2 tablespoons (50g) maple syrup
- ¼ teaspoon (1g) ground Cinnamon
- ½ cup peanuts, finely chopped
- 3 tablespoon (40g) lactose free milk

Process

1. In the bowl of a food processor, combine peanut butter, protein isolate, flour, maple syrup, vanilla, milk and cinnamon

2. Blitz until a dough forms, then form balls using palm of hands
3. Place balls into fridge to firm up.
4. Enjoy after workout or as a light snack

Zucchini and Carrot Slice

Preparation: 10 minutes

Cooking: 35 minutes

Makes: 16 slices

Low FODMAP serving: 1-2 slices

Ingredients

- 2 medium carrots, peeled, grated
- 1 medium zucchini, grated
- 2 spring onions (green part only), finely chopped
- 100g sliced leg ham, finely chopped
- 1 cup (100g) grated tasty cheese
- 1 cup (150g) all Purpose/ Plain Flour

- ¼ cup (7g) chopped fresh flat-leaf parsley leaves
- 4 XL (220g) eggs, lightly beaten
- ¼ cup (55g, 1.9 oz.) lactose free milk
- ¼ cup (60g, 2.1 oz.) vegetable oil
- 1 teaspoon (5g) garlic infused oil (optional)
- Salt and pepper to taste

Process

1. Preheat oven to 160°C fan-forced (320°F). Grease an 18cm x 28cm rectangular brownie/slice pan. Line base and sides with baking paper, allowing sides to overhang.
2. Combine carrot, zucchini, spring onion, ham, cheese, parsley, flour in a large mixing bowl. Stir until well combined then stir in the eggs, milk and oils. Season with salt and pepper.
3. Pour mixtures into the prepared pan, evenly spreading the top with a spatula. Bake for 30-

35 Minutes or until firm. Set aside to cool then cut into squares.

Other Recipes
Chocolate Cardamom Easter Buns

Preparation: 1 hour

Cooking: 10 minutes

Makes: 12-14

Low FODMAP serving: 1 bun

Ingredients

For the buns

- 3 cups (420g) All Purpose/ Plain Flour
- 1 pinch sea salt
- 1 teaspoon ground cardamom seeds
- teaspoon (7g) dry yeast
- ¼ cups (50g) caster sugar
- 1 cup (225mL) lactose free milk

- 70g salted butter

For the filling

- 50g salted butter, softened
- 1 tablespoon caster sugar
- 75g dark chocolate, finely chopped
- For the topping
- 1 egg, lightly beaten
- 1 tablespoon crushed hazelnuts

Process

1. Sift flour into a large bowl and add the salt and freshly ground cardamom. Make a well in the center of the flour and add the yeast.
2. Place butter, milk and sugar in a small saucepan and gently heat to a lukewarm temperature, so the butter is just melted but not hot to touch. Remove from the heat and pour over the yeast.

3. Gently stir the wet mixture with your hands and slowly incorporate the flour. Continue to mix, and then knead to form soft dough. Cover the bowl with glad wrap and a blanket, and place in a warm place to rest for an hour.
4. In a small bowl combine the softened butter and sugar for the filling, and finely chop the chocolate.
5. On a well-floured surface, stretch and roll the dough into a large square, approximately 40x40cm and 1/2 cm thick. Spread the butter evenly across the surface of the dough, and sprinkle with chocolate.
6. Fold the dough into overlapping thirds so you now have a 40x15cm rectangle. Cut the dough into 2-3cm long strips. Carefully picking up one strip at a time, stretch the strip, twisting at the same time and tie into a loose knot shape bun.

7. Place the buns on a tray lined with baking paper, cover and allow it to rest for 30 minutes. Preheat oven to 220°C (428oF) and once the buns have rested, brush each with the egg wash and sprinkle with hazelnuts. Bake for 8-10 minutes or until golden.

Chocolate Pound Cake

Preparation: 15 minutes

Cooking: 30 minutes

Makes: 1 large loaf of cake

Low FODMAP serving: 1 slice - 2 slices

Ingredients

- 225g salted butter, softened
- ½ cup caster sugar
- ½ cup brown sugar
- 4 eggs
- 1.5 cups Baking Mix

- ¼ cup cocoa
- 2 teaspoon baking powder
- 1 pinch salt

For the icing

- 50g butter, salted
- 1.5 cups icing sugar
- 1 tablespoon cocoa
- Dash almond milk

Process

1. Preheat the oven to 180°C (356°F) and grease a standard (23x13cm) loaf tin.
2. In a large mixing bowl, cream together the softened butter and the sugars until smooth.
3. Add the eggs and whisk until well combined.
4. Sift in the four, cacao powder, baking powder and salt and mix until a smooth and even batter forms.

5. Pour the batter in the loaf tin and even it out with a spatula.
6. Bake in the oven for 30 minutes or until risen, pulled away from the sides and an inserted skewer comes out clean.
7. Leave the cake in the tin for 5 minutes before turning it out onto a wire rack to cool.
8. While the cake is cooling, make the icing by whisking together all the icing ingredients until smooth and fluffy. Spread evenly over the cake.

Citrus Pound Cake

Preparation: 15 minutes

Cooking: 30 Minutes

Makes: 1 large loaf of cake

Low FODMAP serving: 1 slice

Ingredients

- 225g salted butter, softened
- 1 cup caster sugar
- 3 eggs
- ½ orange juice and zest
- 1 ¾ cups Baking Mix
- 2 teaspoon baking powder
- 1 pinch salt

For the glaze

- 1.5 cups freshly squeezed orange juice
- 1 lemon juice

- ½ cup caster sugar

Process

1. Preheat the oven to 160°C (320°F) and grease a standard (23x13cm) loaf tin.
2. In a large mixing bowl, cream together the softened butter and the sugars until smooth.
3. Add the eggs, orange juice and zest and whisk until well combined.
4. Sift in the flour, baking powder and salt and mix until a smooth and even batter forms.
5. Pour the batter in the loaf tin and even it out with a spatula.
6. Bake in the oven for 30 minutes or until risen, pulled away from the sides and an inserted skewer comes out clean.
7. While the cake is cooking, make the syrup by combining the orange and lemon juice and caster sugar in a saucepan over medium heat until thickened.

8. Leave the cake in the tin for 5 minutes before turning it out onto a wire rack to cool.
9. Once cool, drizzle the glaze over the cake and serve.

Condensed Milk Pound Cake

Preparation: 20 minutes

Cooking: 30 minutes

Makes: 1 loaf of cake

Low FODMAP serving: 1 slice

Ingredients

For the condensed milk

- 100g coconut milk powder
- ½ cup caster sugar
- 1 tablespoon coconut oil
- ¼ cup boiling water

For the cake

- 100g Coconut condensed milk from above
- 120g butter, softened
- ¾ cup caster sugar
- 3 eggs
- 1 ¾ cup Baking Mix
- 2 teaspoon baking powder
- 1 pinch salt

Process

1. Preheat the oven to 160°C (320°F) and grease a standard (23x13cm) loaf tin.
2. In a blender, combine the ingredients for the Condensed Milk until thick and glossy.
3. In a large mixing bowl, cream together 100 grams of the Condensed Milk you've just prepared, the softened butter and sugar until smooth.
4. Add the eggs and whisk until well combined.

5. Sift in the flour, baking powder and salt and mix until a smooth and even batter forms.
6. Pour the batter in the loaf tin and even it out with a spatula.
7. Bake in the oven for 30 minutes or until risen, pulled away from the sides and an inserted skewer comes out clean.
8. Leave the cake in the tin for 5 minutes before turning it out onto a wire rack to cool.
9. Once cool, drizzle the remaining Condensed Milk over the cake and serve.

Cinnamon Tea Cupcakes with Meringue Icing

Preparation: 20 minutes

Cooking: 35 minutes

Makes: 8

Low FODMAP serving: 1

Ingredients

For the cupcakes

- 1 cup almond milk
- 1 teaspoon apple cider vinegar
- ¼ cup butter
- ½ cup brown sugar
- ¼ cup caster sugar
- 1 cup Baking Mix
- 1 cup All Purpose/ Plain Flour
- 1 tablespoon ground cinnamon
- 1 pinch salt

- 1 teaspoon vanilla essence

For the icing

- 3 egg whites
- ¾ cup sugar
- 1 teaspoon corn flour

Process

1. Preheat the oven to 180°C fan forced and grease a standard muffin tray.
2. In a large mixing bowl, combine the almond milk and apple cider vinegar and set aside for 5 minutes.
3. Add the melted butter and sugars to the milk mixture and stir to combine.
4. Sift in the flours and cinnamon, and add the salt and vanilla. Whisk until the mixture is smooth
5. Divide the mixture between 8 holes of the muffin tray and bake for 25 minutes or until

cupcakes have shrunk in slightly from the edges of the tray and an inserted skewer comes out clean.
6. Turn the cupcakes out onto a wire rack to cool.
7. To prepare the icing, set up a double boiler over a stove and once boiling, reduce to a simmer.
8. Add the egg whites and sugar to the bowl over the double boiler and whisk continuously until the sugar has dissolved.
9. Remove the bowl from the double boiler and add the corn flour. Beat the mixture until it is thick and glossy and stick peaks have formed.
10. Transfer the meringue icing to a piping bag and pipe on to the cupcakes. Torch the meringue if desired.

Mixed Berry Sponge

Preparation: 15 minutes

Cooking: 15 minutes

Makes: 2 x 15cm cakes or 1 large sponge

Low FODMAP serve: 1 slice

Ingredients

For the sponge

- 4 eggs, divided
- ½ cup caster sugar
- ½ cup Baking Mix
- ¼ cup Purpose/ Plain Flour
- ¼ cup corn flour
- ½ teaspoon bicarbonate of soda
- 1 teaspoon vanilla essence
- 1 pinch salt

For the filling

- 400mL lactose free pouring cream
- 200g mixed berries

Process

1. Preheat the oven to 180°C fan forced and grease 2 x 15cm cake tins, or 1 large cake tin.
2. Sift the flours 3 times into a large bowl to ensure it is aerated and no lumps remain.
3. Beat the egg whites and the caster sugar in a stand mixer on high until soft peaks have formed.
4. Add the egg yolks and beat briefly to incorporate.
5. While continuously beating on a low setting, gradually add the flours, bicarbonate of soda, vanilla and salt until just combined.
6. Divide the batter between the tins and bake in the oven for 15 minutes or until the cakes

are springy to the touch and an inserted skewer comes out clean.
7. Turn the cakes out onto wire racks immediately to cool.
8. Once cool, whip the pouring cream and spread over the middle and top of the cake. Top the cream on each layer with mixed berries and serve immediately.

Carrot Cake Cupcakes

Preparation: 20 minutes

Cooking: 25 minutes

Makes: 10

Low FODMAP serving: 1

Ingredients

For the cupcakes

- 1 cup almond milk
- 1 teaspoon apple cider vinegar

- ¼ cup butter
- ½ cup brown sugar
- ¼ cup caster sugar
- 1 cup All Purpose/ Plain Flour
- 1 cup Baking Mix
- ½ tablespoon ground cinnamon
- 180g shredded carrot
- 100g walnuts
- 1 pinch salt
- 1 teaspoon vanilla essence

For the icing

- 70g smooth ricotta
- 30g butter
- 2 ½ cups icing sugar

Process

1. Preheat the oven to 180°C fan forced and grease a standard muffin tray.

2. In a large mixing bowl, combine the almond milk and apple cider vinegar and set aside for 5 minutes.
3. Meanwhile, peel and shred the carrots and roughly chop the walnuts
4. Add the melted butter and sugars to the milk mixture and stir to combine.
5. Sift in the flours and cinnamon, and add the salt and vanilla. Whisk until the mixture is smooth.
6. Add the shredded carrot and chopped walnuts and fold through until evenly incorporated.
7. Divide the mixture between 10 holes of the muffin tray and bake for 25 minutes or until cupcakes have shrunk in slightly from the edges of the tray and an inserted skewer comes out clean.
8. Turn the cupcakes out onto a wire rack to cool.

9. To prepare the icing, place the butter and ricotta in a large mixing bowl and cream together using an electric whisk.
10. Add the icing sugar and whisk until a smooth buttercream forms.
11. Spread or pipe the icing onto the cupcakes.

St Clements Bundt Cake

Preparation: 15 minutes

Cooking: 45 minutes

Makes: 6-8 servings

Low FODMAP servings: 1

Ingredients

For the cake

- ½ orange zest and juice
- 1 lemon zest and juice
- 1 teaspoon vanilla paste
- 1 cup (220g) caster sugar

- 250g unsalted butter, softened
- 4 eggs
- 2 ¼ cups (335g) all Purpose/ Plain Flour
- ½ cup lactose free sour cream
- 1 pinch sea salt

For the drizzle icing

- 1 lemon zest and juice
- 2 cups icing sugar

Process

1. Preheat oven to 180°C and grease your favorite bundt tin.
2. Combine the zest, sugar and butter in the bowl of an electric mixer with a paddle attachment. Cream until pale and fluffy (about five minutes).
3. Add the eggs, one at a time, beating well between each addition.

4. Add half of the dry ingredients, and the vanilla, and beat on low speed until just combined. Add half of the sour cream and the lemon and orange juice and slowly beat again. Repeat with remaining dry ingredients and sour cream.
5. Bake for 45 minutes, or until the sides of the cake are just pulling away from the tin and a skewer comes out clean. Let cool in the tin for five minutes, then turn out onto a wire rack to cool completely.
6. For the icing, sift the icing sugar into a bowl and add the zest and juice, a little at a time, stirring well as you go. The icing needs to be quite thick so it doesn't dribble all the way down the cake.
7. Once the cake is completely cool, gently pour thick icing over the top of the cake, allowing it to freely and slowly drizzle down the sides

Lemon, Yogurt and Lemon Thyme Bundt Cake

Preparation: 10 minutes

Cooking: 35 minutes

Makes: 1 cake, 8 servings

Low FODMAP serving: 1

Ingredients

For the bundt

- 180g butter, melted
- 2 zest of 2 lemons
- ½ juice of half a lemon
- 1 cup low fat Greek yogurt
- 3 eggs
- 2 cups All Purpose/ Plain Flour
- 1 ½ cups caster sugar
- 2 teaspoon baking powder

- 1 tablespoon plus extra to serve lemon thyme

For the icing

- 1 cup icing sugar
- 1 zest and juice of 1 lemon
- Lactose free milk - as needed

Process

1. Preheat oven to 180C and grease a bundt or regular 24 cm spring form cake tin.
2. Mix together the butter and sugar, then add the lemon zest and lemon thyme.
3. Add the flour and baking powder to your sugar mixture, and then add the eggs one at a time until well combined.
4. Fold in the Greek yogurt and lemon juice, then Pour mixture into the prepared cake tin and bake for 35 minutes or until golden brown and just firm to touch.

5. Let cool in the tin for 5 minutes before turning out to a cooling rack. To make the icing whisk together icing sugar, lemon juice and add milk until you have a thick smooth icing.
6. Once cake is completely cool pour this over the top, letting the icing drizzle down the sides.
7. Decorate with a few extra lemon thyme leaves.

Chocolate Bundt with Ganache

Preparation: 15 minutes

Cooking: 45 minutes

Makes: 6-8 serves

Low FODMAP serving: 1

Ingredients

For the bundt

- ¾ cup (75g) cocoa
- 1 teaspoon salt
- 2 ¼ cups (335g) all Purpose/ Plain Flour
- 2 teaspoon baking powder
- 220g unsalted butter, softened
- 1 ½ cups (330g) caster sugar
- ½ cup (135g) lactose free sour cream
- 4 eggs
- 1 teaspoon vanilla extract

For the ganache

- 100g dark chocolate
- ½ cup (125mLs) lactose free heavy cream
- 2 tablespoon butter

Process

1. Preheat oven to 180C and grease your favorite bundt tin.
2. Place the cocoa powder, salt, flour and baking powder in a large bowl and whisk to combine.
3. Place the butter and sugar in the bowl of an electric mixer and cream until pale and fluffy, about five minutes. Add the eggs, beating well after each addition.
4. Add half of the dry ingredients, and the vanilla, and beat on low speed until just combined. Add half of the sour cream and slowly beat again. Repeat with remaining dry ingredients and sour cream.

5. Transfer to your prepared bundt tin and smooth the surface with the back of a spoon or offset spatula. Bake for about 45 minutes or until a skewer comes out clean.
6. Transfer to a wire rack to cool for five minutes before carefully removing cake from the pan (see note).
7. For the ganache, place cream in a small saucepan and bring just to simmering point.
8. Remove from heat, add butter and chocolate and stir until smooth and slightly thickened.
9. Transfer to a jug and leave to thicken a little further for at least 10 minutes. Pour over cooled bundt.

Vegan Blueberry Pancakes

Preparation: 5 minutes

Cooking: 5 minutes

Makes: 12

Low FODMAP serving: 1

Ingredients

- 2 cups Baking Mix
- 1 ½ cup almond milk
- 1 tablespoon maple syrup
- 1 teaspoon vanilla essence
- 250 g blueberries
- Cooking oil

Process

1. In a mixing bowl, whisk together the almond milk and baking mix flour.

2. Add in the maple syrup, vanilla and whisk to combine.
3. Heat a pan on medium heat and grease with a cooking spray.
4. Pour ¼ cup of pancake dough in the pan, and then add a few blueberries per pancake. Cook on one side until bubbles form then flip and cook the other side pressing slightly for 1-2 minutes.
5. Keep going with the reminder of the pancake dough.

Vegan Chocolate Peanut Butter Cookies

Preparation: 15 minutes

Cooking: 10 minutes

Makes: 16

Low FODMAP serving: 1

Ingredients

- 1 cup all Purpose/ Plain Flour
- ½ cup smooth peanut butter
- ⅓ Cup cacao or cocoa powder
- ⅓ Cup maple syrup
- ¼ cup coconut oil
- ¼ cup almond milk

Process

1. Preheat your oven to 180C (356F) and line a baking tray with baking paper.

2. In a bowl combine the flour, cacao, and maple syrup
3. Then add the almond milk and melted coconut oil and combine.
4. Finish by folding the peanut butter with the chocolate cookie dough – purposely not mixing it fully together to leave peanut butter swirls.
5. Roll the dough with your hands to form balls, place on the baking tray and press down with a fork.
6. Place them in the oven and bake for 10 minutes.

Vegan Beetroot Brownies

Preparation: 20 minutes

Cooking: 30 minutes

Makes: 16

Low FODMAP serving: 1

Ingredients

- 250g cooked beetroot
- 1 cup Baking Mix
- 1 tablespoon flax meal
- 3 tablespoon water
- ¾ cup maple syrup
- ½ cup almond milk
- ½ cup cocoa powder
- 1 teaspoon baking powder

Process

1. Preheat your oven to 180 C (356F) and line a brownie tin with baking paper.
2. In a small bowl create the flax eggs by whisking together the flax meal and water. Then leave to set.
3. In a blender or food processor blend the cooked beetroots to form a beetroot puree.
4. In a mixing bowl, combine the flour, beetroot puree, flax eggs, maple syrup, cocoa, almond milk, and baking powder. Whisk until there are no lumps.
5. Pour mixture into your brownie tin and place in the oven to bake for 30 minutes.
6. Sprinkle cacao over the top before cutting and serving.

Chocolate Chip Monster Cookies

Preparation: 15 minutes

Cooking: 8 minutes

Makes: 8

Low FODMAP serving: 1

Ingredients

- 50g butter
- ¼ cup coconut oil
- ¼ cup almond milk
- 1 tablespoon cocoa
- 1 cup Baking Mix
- ½ cup almond meal
- ½ cup chocolate chips
- ½ cup brown sugar

Process

1. Preheat the oven to 160°C (320°F) fan forced and line a baking tray with grease proof paper.
2. In a large, microwave safe mixing bowl, melt the butter and coconut oil together in the microwave.
3. Add the almond milk and cacao powder and whisk until well incorporated.
4. Add the brown sugar, Baking Mix and the almond meal and mix until a smooth dough forms.
5. Roll the dough out into 8 balls and distribute them evenly on the tray. Place a handful of chocolate chips onto the top of each ball so when they bake the colors stay at the top.
6. Bake the cookies in the oven for approximately 8 minutes. Leave them on the tray to cool before storing in an airtight container.

Spooky Halloween Brownies

Preparation: 10 minutes

Baking: 25 minutes

Makes: 12

Low FODMAP serving: 1-2

Ingredients

- 100g dark chocolate
- 100g butter
- ½ teaspoon vanilla essence
- 2 eggs
- ½ cup all Purpose/ Plain Flour
- 1 cup sugar
- 1 pinch salt

For the topping

- 125g butter
- 1 ½ cups icing sugar

- 1 tablespoon lactose free milk
- ¼ cup chocolate chips

Process

1. Heat oven to 180°C (356°F) and line a 20 cm brownie pan with parchment paper.
2. Melt chocolate and butter in a small pot on a low heat. Transfer chocolate and butter mixture to a large bowl and stir in sugar and vanilla essence. Once combined, beat in eggs one at a time. Gently fold in the flour.
3. Transfer mixture to lined brownie pan and bake for 20-25 minutes. For a gooey brownie, you want the Brownie to form a crust but be not quite set in the middle. Remove from the oven and allow it to cool down.
4. Once brownie has cooled, make the white buttercream icing by combining the butter and sugar with an electric mixer. Add the

lactose free milk as you need to achieve a lovely thick texture.
5. Once the brownies have completely cooled, slice them up into individual pieces.
6. Fill a zip lock bag with your buttercream icing and pip stripes over your brownies like the bandages on a mummy.
7. Add two buttercream icing dots for eyed and top with two chocolate chips.

Choc Hot Cross Buns

Preparation: 40 minutes

Cooking: 25 minutes

Makes: 10-12

Low FODMAP serving: 1

Ingredients

For the buns

- 14 g dry yeast
- 350 mL lactose free milk
- 80 mL canola oil
- ½ cup sugar
- 1 egg
- 4 cups all Purpose/ Plain Flour
- 2 tablespoon cocoa powder
- 1 tablespoon mixed spice
- 1 tablespoon ground cinnamon
- ½ cup chocolate chips

For the cross

- ⅔ cup all Purpose/ Plain Flour
- ½ teaspoon ground cinnamon
- ¼ cup caster sugar
- ½ cup water

For the glaze

- 40g sugar
- 1 orange zest and juice
- 2 tablespoon water

Process

1. Place yeast in a large bowl and add the milk, whisk together and let sit for 10 minutes or until mixture is frothy.
2. In a small jug, mix the oil, sugar and egg together then add this to the yeasted milk.
3. Now add the flour, cocoa and spices and bring mixture together to form dough.

4. Tip out onto a work surface and knead for 6 minutes or until the dough is smooth and stretchy.
5. About halfway into the kneading process, add the chocolate chips so they are evenly incorporated into the dough.
6. Lightly oil your mixing bowl then place the dough back into it and cover with a clean tea towel. Let rest for one hour or until the dough has doubled in size.
7. Tear off a small amount of the dough, about the size of a small apple and gently shape into a round ball.
8. Place this on a shallow baking tray lined with paper and repeat with remaining dough.
9. Let the shaped buns rest for a further half an hour.
10. Preheat oven to 200oC (392oF).
11. To make the piping mixture, combine the flour, cinnamon, sugar and water in a small

bowl and whisk until you have a thick paste, add a little more flour or water as needed.
12. Spoon mixture into a small plastic bag, snip off the bottom and slowly pipe a cross on top of the buns.
13. Place in the oven for 25 minutes or until buns are cooked through.
14. Towards the end of your cooking time, combine glaze ingredients in a small saucepan over medium heat, cook until sugar has dissolved and you have thick syrup.
15. As soon as the buns come out of the oven, brush the glaze generously over the top of each bun. Let cool a little then serve as is or with a smear of butter and a little jam

Chicken Tortilla's

Preparation: 1 hour

Cooking: 20 minutes

Makes: 8 wraps

Low FODMAP serving: 2 wraps

Ingredients

For the wraps

- 2 cups all Purpose/ Plain Flour
- ¾ cup water
- 1 teaspoon salt
- 3 tablespoon olive oil

For the filling

- 2 teaspoon smoked paprika
- 1 teaspoon cumin
- 1 teaspoon oregano
- ½ teaspoon chili powder

- 1 tablespoon garlic infused oil
- 500g chicken breast

To serve

- To serve tomato
- To serve spinach or lettuce
- 1tbs (max per serve) sour cream

Process

1. In a large bowl combine the flour and salt. Make a well in the center and add in the water and olive oil. Use a spoon or your hands to bring the mixture together.
2. Tip out onto a floured surface and knead for 5 minutes until it forms a smooth ball.
3. Place the dough back in the bowl and cover and allow it to rest on the bench for 20-30 minutes.
4. Meanwhile prepare the filling. Slice each chicken breast into 4 pieces. Then in a bowl

mix them with remaining spices and oil, allow to marinate for 30 minutes.

5. Preheat a fry pan. Once the dough has rested cut it into 8 even pieces. On slightly floured surface roll one piece of dough out to 2-3 mm thick and 7-8 inches in diameter.
6. Carefully pick up the dough piece and flip it onto the hot pan. Cook for 1 min; it should begin to puff up. Flip it over and cook for another 30 sec-1 min.
7. Remove from pan and repeat with remaining dough. Wrap the cooked tortillas in a clean tea towel or aluminum foil to keep them warm until ready to eat.
8. Preheat a large fry pan and then cook the chicken for 3 minutes on each side to brown. Pour ¼ cup water to the pan and then place a lid on the fry pan and cook for another 7-10 minutes or until chicken is cooked through.

9. Remove the chicken from the pan and allow it to cool slightly before using two forks to shred the chicken.
10. Prepare any other fillings you want for your tortillas – diced tomatoes, shredded lettuce, sour cream and sliced jalapenos are also good

Chunky Beef Pie

Preparation: 1 hour

Cooking: 2 hours

Makes: 1 pie with 8 servings

Low FODMAP serving: 1 Serving

Ingredients

For the pastry

- 300 g all Purpose/ Plain Flour
- 1 teaspoon salt
- 125 g cold butter, cubed
- 130 g ice cold water
- 1 egg
- 1 teaspoon baking powder

For the filling

- 1kg gravy or chuck beef, diced
- 2 tablespoon all Purpose/ Plain Flour

- 4 tablespoon olive oil
- 1 leek, green part only thinly chopped
- 1 pinch salt and pepper
- 1 heaped teaspoon tomato paste
- 2 cups low FODMAP beef stock
- 1 sprig rosemary
- 1 sprig thyme

Process

1. If possible make the filling the day before, or at least a few hours before completing the pie so that it can cool completely.
2. To make the filling, toss the beef in the flour. Heat the oil and brown half of the meat in the pan, then remove and brown the other half. Set the beef aside.
3. Sauté the leek for about 2 minutes until soft and then add the meat back into the pan. Stir in the remaining ingredients. Bring to the boil and then reduce to a simmer for 1 hour

or until meat starts to fall apart. Stir occasionally to prevent sticking.

4. To make the pastry, combine the flour and salt in a large bowl. Using your hands, rub the butter into the flour to form a rough crumb.
5. Add in the water in 1 tbsp. at a time until it comes together. Tip out onto a floured surface and knead for 5-10 minutes until it becomes smooth Steep
6. Try not to add too much extra flour to the mixture. Cover dough and then let it rest in the fridge for at least 30 minutes. The pastry can be made the day before, but remove from fridge 1 hour before to allow it to become malleable.
7. To construct the pie, preheat the oven to 180C.
8. Cut the pastry in half and then roll out the first piece on a floured surface until it is ¼

inch thick. Place it in the pie dish, molding to the shape and then use a sharp knife to trim the sides.
9. Spread the filling into the base. Whisk the egg with a fork and then brush the edges of the base with the egg. Top with the second piece of pastry and use your thumb or a fork to press down on the edges to seal the pie.

Pita Pockets with Pumpkin and Walnut Dip

Preparation: 1 hour

Resting: 2 hours

Cooking: 20 minutes

Makes: 12

Low FODMAP serving: 2

Ingredients

For the pita

- 320g warm water
- 20g caster sugar
- 1.5 teaspoon (7g) dry yeast
- 525g Baking Mix
- ½ teaspoon salt
- 15-20g olive oil

For the dip

- 700g Japanese or Kent pumpkin (only)
- 1 tablespoon olive oil
- ½ cup Greek yogurt
- ½ cup walnuts
- ½ cup parsley, finely chopped
- 2 teaspoon paprika
- ½ teaspoon ground coriander
- 1 teaspoon cumin
- Salt and pepper to taste

Process

1. In a small bowl add the yeast and sugar to the warm water – it should just be warm to touch as if it is too hot it will kill the yeast. Set aside for 10 minutes to allow the yeast to bloom.
2. In a large bowl combine the flour and salt. Make a well in the center and carefully pour in the yeast mixture. Use your hands or a

wooden spoon to bring the flour and yeast mixture together to form soft dough.
3. Tip out onto a floured surface and knead for 2-3 minutes until the dough begins to spring back.
4. Oil your bowl and place the dough back into the bowl, covering with a tea towel or cling wrap. Set aside in a warm place in your house to rise for 2 hrs. Until doubled in size.
5. Preheat the oven to 250 C and place a tray on the center rack in the oven to heat up.
6. Once the dough has risen, punch it down to remove all of the gas bubbles. Then tip it out onto a floured surface.
7. Divide the dough into 12 even pieces (each pita should weigh around 80g); cover them with a damp tea towel so they don't dry out. Roll one piece of dough to about 7 inches wide and ¼ inches thick.

8. Carefully pick it up and flip it onto the hot tray. Cook for 2-3 minutes. It should inflate – which is a sign it is ready.
9. Cover with a tea towel once cooked so they stay warm, or if you want to enjoy them later, once cool place them in a zip lock plastic bag to stay soft.
10. To make the dip, preheat the oven to 200C. Peel the pumpkin and cut into 2 inch chunks. Then place on a baking tray and drizzle with olive oil. Cook in the oven for 20 minutes or until just soft. Allow to cool for 10 minutes.
11. Place the walnuts into the food processor and blitz for 1 min or until they form a fine crumb. Add in remaining ingredients and blitz for 1-2 minutes or until smooth and creamy.

Gnocchi

Preparation: 20 minutes

Cooking: 1 hour

Makes: 1 kg

Ingredients

For the Gnocchi

- 1kg potato
- 350g Plain Flour
- 1 pinch freshly ground nutmeg
- 1 teaspoon sea salt
- 2 eggs

For the sage and butter sauce

- 100g butter
- 1 lemon zest
- 1 pinch salt and pepper
- 10 leaves sage

For simple tomato sauce

- 600g tinned plum tomatoes
- 1 handful basil leaves
- 4 Tbsps. olive oil
- 1 Pinch salt
- 2 Tbsps. garlic infused oil

Process

1. Preheat oven to 160oC (320oF).
2. Wash the potatoes (but don't peel), dry well and prick all over the potatoes. Place in the oven and cook for an hour or until tender.
3. While the potatoes are still hot, slice them in half and scoop out the insides into a bowl. Using a potato rice or wire sieve, 'rice' the potatoes.
4. Add most of the flour (reserving 1/2 cup), nutmeg and sea salt and gently mix together with your fingers.
5. Make a well in the center and add the eggs.

6. Working it gently, bring everything together into dough. Make sure not to overwork the dough to ensure your gnocchi is pillow soft.
7. Once the dough is dry enough to work with, dust your work surface with the remaining flour and divide the dough into four pieces.
8. Roll each piece of dough into a long sausage, about 3-4cm wide. Cut 2cm 'gnocchi pieces' out. Press each 'gnocchi' piece against the inside of a fork and your thumb, then lightly dust with flour and place on a tray lined with baking paper.
9. You can now either freeze the gnocchi (they can be cooked from frozen) or drop them straight into a big pot of salted boiling water and cook until they have all bubbled up to the surface of the water and then count to five before draining the water. Either freeze the gnocchi to be cooked later or place the pieces straight into a pot of salted boiling

water. Cook the gnocchi until they have bubbled up to the surface of the water and drain.
10. For the Sage and butter sauce: Melt the butter until almost browned, add the sage leaves and lemon zest and cook for another couple of minutes. Poor over the gnocchi and grate over parmesan cheese to serve.

Cheese Straws

Preparation: 30 minutes

Baking: 20 minutes

Makes: 10 – 12 Cheese straw

Low FODMAP serve: 2 Straw

Ingredients

- 1 cup (140g) all Purpose Flour
- ½ cup (50g) Grated Mozzarella
- 1-2 tablespoon (10g) Grated Parmesan

- ½ cup (115g) Unsalted Butter, softened and cut into cubes
- ½ teaspoon (1.5g) paprika
- ¼ teaspoon (7g) salt
- 1 tablespoon (15g) water
- 1 tablespoon (15g) Lactose Free Milk

Process

1. Preheat fan-forced oven to 205°C (400°F).
2. Combine all the ingredients except milk in a bowl and bring together with your hands until breadcrumb like dough forms.
3. Place in freezer for 10 minutes to cool mixture down.
4. Remove from freezer and add milk, kneading until a soft dough forms.
5. Roll out dough into a rectangular shape of a desired thickness then cut into 12 straws.
6. Place each straw onto a baking tray and bake for 15-20 minutes or until golden brown.

Pretzels

Preparation: 30 minutes

Resting: 1 hour

Baking: 15 minutes

Makes: 4 – 6 pretzels

Low FODMAP serve: 1 pretzel

Ingredients

- 2 ⅓ cup (330g) all Purpose Flour, plus more for kneading
- 1 cup (240g) Lactose Free Milk
- 3 tablespoon (45g) brown sugar
- 1 ½ (9g) dry yeast
- 2 tablespoon (28g) unsalted butter
- 1 teaspoon (7g) salt
- ⅓ cup (60g) baking soda

Process

1. Warm the milk in a microwave until lukewarm, and then add the dry yeast. Sit for 2 minutes.
2. Add the brown sugar, 2 cups of flour and mix with a wooden spoon. Add the melted butter and mix further.
3. Add the remaining 1/3 cup flour and salt to produce sticky dough.
4. Transfer the dough to a lightly floured work surface.
5. Knead the dough, (add more flour if the dough is too difficult to handle), for about 5 minutes.
6. Place the dough into a bowl and cover with tea towel, allow it to rest for 60 minutes.
7. Preheat fan-forced oven to 230°C (450°F) and prepare a baking tray with baking paper.
8. Move the dough back onto your floured work surface and punch to deflate.

9. Divide dough into 6 pieces, roll and stretch each piece with palms of your hand into 60 centimeter (30 inch) ropes.
10. Form each rope into a pretzel shape.
11. Dissolve baking soda with 3 cups of warm water; use this mix to lightly brush the pretzels.
12. Bake pretzels for approximately 12-15 minutes depending on their thickness.
13. Cool on a wired rack.

Chicken and Tomato Pasta Sauce

Preparation: 10 minutes

Cooking: 10 minutes

Makes: 4 servings

Low FODMAP serving: 1 serving

Ingredients

- 400g (14oz) chicken breast, sliced thinly
- Garlic infused olive oil
- 1 red capsicum (bell pepper), cut into 3cm x 3 cm cubes
- 1 punnet cherry tomatoes, halved
- 1 ½ cup tomato passata
- 100-200g (3.4–6.8oz) low FODMAP chicken stock
- ½ cup basil

Process

1. Heat a large frying pan over medium heat and add the garlic infused olive oil. Once hot, add the chicken breast and cook through. Add the bell pepper and cherry tomatoes and sauté for 2 minutes.
2. Add the passata and chicken stock. Allow the sauce to reduce slightly (add more stock if needed), and then add drained pasta to the frying pan and mix it through the sauce.
3. Serve the pasta warm with fresh basil.

Sausage Rolls

Preparation: 1 hour

Baking: 20 minutes

Makes: 8 – 10 sausage rolls

Low FODMAP serve: 2 sausage rolls

Ingredients

For Rough-Puff Pastry

- 1 ¾ cup (250g) all Purpose/Plain Flour
- 1 ½ cup (250g) Unsalted Butter, softened
- ¾ cup (180g) chilled water
- 1 teaspoon (7g) salt
- For Sausage filling
- ¼ cup (30g) all Purpose/Plain Flour
- 450g beef mince
- ½ cup (40g) Green portion of shallots
- 1 teaspoon (7g) salt
- 1 teaspoon (3g) ground black pepper

- ¼ cup (60g) Vegetable oil
- 2 XL (55g) eggs beaten

Process

1. Sift the flour and salt into a large bowl.
2. Rub diced butter into the flour until a sandy consistency.
3. Make a well in the middle of the mixture and add 2/3 of the water into the mix, add more water if the dough is too sticky.
4. Cover the dough with cling wrap and let rest for 30 minutes in the fridge.
5. Transfer the dough onto a lightly floured work surface.
6. Knead the dough gently until it comes together.
7. Roll out into rectangle shapes, folding in half, and rolling out again.
8. Repeat folding step five times, and then transfer back into the fridge for 20 minutes.

9. Preheat fan-forced oven to 205°C (400°F).
10. Meanwhile, in a large bowl add lean beef mince, shallots, oil, salt and pepper, flour and one egg; mix by hand until well combined.
11. Remove pastry from the fridge, divide into half and roll into 2 long rectangles, at least 60 centimeters (24 inches) long and 20 centimeters (8 inches) wide. Trim the edges to create neat borders.
12. Spoon mixture into the center of the rectangles to create long sausage. Use a pastry brush to brush egg where the pastry joins.
13. Divide the sausages into 4-5 pieces and transfer onto baking tray with baking sheet. Brush the top with egg wash.
14. Bake for 20 minutes or until golden brown.
15. Allow to cool prior to consumption.

A comprehensive table for some foods and their FODMAPs

Fruits	Fructose	Fructans	GOS	Lactose	Polyols
Apple	✓				✓
Apricot (1 or less)					✓
Apricot (1 or more)		✓			✓
Avocado (more than 1/8)					✓
Blackberry					✓
Boysenberry	✓				
Cherry	✓				✓
Custard apple			✓		
Fig (dried)		✓			
Fig (fresh)	✓				
Grapefruit		✓			
Longan					✓
Lychee					✓
Mango	✓				
Nectarine		✓			✓
Peach (yellow)					✓
Peach (white)		✓			✓
Peach (clingstone)					✓
Pear	✓				✓
Persimmon		✓			
Plum		✓			✓

	Fructose	Fructans	GOS	Lactose	Polyols
Prune		✓			✓
Canned fruit in natural juice	✓				
watermelon	✓	✓			✓

Dairy	Fructose	Fructans	GOS	Lactose	Polyols
Cottage cheese				✓	
Cream cheese				✓	
Custard				✓	
Dry milk solids				✓	
Gelato				✓	
Goat's milk				✓	
Ice cream				✓	
Mascarpone				✓	
Milk (from cows, goats, sheep)				✓	
Ricotta cheese				✓	
Yogurt				✓	
Oat milk			✓		
Rice milk		✓	✓		

Vegetables	Fructose	Fructans	GOS	Lactose	Polyols
Artichoke (globe)		✓			
Artichoke (hearts)	✓				
Asparagus	✓	✓	✓		
Beetroot (more than 2 slices)		✓	✓		
Broccoli (more than ½ cup)		✓	✓		✓
Brussels sprouts (more than ½ cup)		✓			
Butternut squash (more than ¼ cup)			✓		
Cabbage (savoy)		✓			
Cauliflower					✓
Celery (more than ½ stalk)					✓
Corn (more than ½ cob)			✓		✓
Fennel (more than 1 cup)		✓			✓
Garlic		✓			
Leek		✓			

Mushrooms					✓
Okra (more than 10 pods)		✓			
Onion (all)		✓			
Pumpkin (canned, more than ½ cup)		✓	✓		✓
Shallots		✓			

Snow peas (more than 5 pods)		✓	✓		✓
Spring onion (whole)		✓			
Sugar snap peas	✓				
Sweet potato (more than ½ cup)					✓

Tomato paste	✓				

Grains	Fructose	Fructans	GOS	Lactose	Polyols
All-purpose flour		✓			
Barley		✓	✓		
Bulgur wheat		✓			
Couscous		✓			
Kamut		✓			
Pasta		✓			
Rye	✓	✓	✓		
Wheat		✓			
Wheat berries		✓			

Legumes & Nuts	Fructose	Fructans	GOS	Lactose	Polyols
Almond (more than 10 nuts)			✓		
Baked bean		✓	✓		

Cashew		✓	✓		
Chickpea (more than ¼ cup)			✓		
Hazelnut (more than 10 nuts)		✓	✓		
Kidney bean		✓	✓		
Lentil (more than ½ cup)		✓	✓		
Pistachio		✓	✓		
Soy bean		✓	✓		
Soy milk (from whole soy bean)		✓	✓		

Beverages	Fructose	Fructans	GOS	Lactose	Polyols
Chamomile tea		✓			
Chia tea		✓			
Dandelion tea		✓			
Fennel tea		✓			
Oolong tea		✓			

Rum	✓				

Sugar	Fructose	Fructans	GOS	Lactose	Polyols
Agave syrup	✓				
Crystalline fructose	✓				
Erythriol*					✓
Fructo-oligosaccharides (fos)		✓			
Fractose	✓				
Fractose solids	✓				
Fruit juice concentrate	✓				
Glycerin/glycerol					✓
High fructose corn syrup	✓				
Honey	✓				

Isomalt						✓
Lactitol						✓
Maltitol						✓
Mannitol						✓
Molasses	✓					
Polydextrose						✓
Sorbitol						✓
Xylitol						✓

others	Fructose	Fructans	GOS	Lactose	Polyols
carb		✓			
Chicory root extract		✓			
Cocoa powder (more than 1 Tbsp)		✓	✓		
Inulin		✓			

Natural flavor (in savory foods)		✓			
Textured vegetable protein				✓	

Printed in Great Britain
by Amazon